TABLE OF CONTENTS

Introduction

Bee products are natural substances that are either gathered and processed by bees, such as nectar, pollen from flowers, and resin, or are released by the bees themselves through glands, such as venom, wax, and royal jelly. A ffluence of studies on bee products, such as honey, propolis, royal jelly, bee bread, and bee pollen, have been conducted in recent years as a result of research trends for bioactive compounds of natural origin. Due to beekeepers' lack of knowledge of the proper technique for gathering this product without completely damaging the hive until a few years ago, bee bread is a unique bee product that is not well recognized.

The two primary sources of nutrition for honey bees that are required for colony population health maintenance and survival are: both flower pollen and nectar/honeydew. Carbohydrates are provided by nectar and honeydew, while pollen also contains lipids, proteins, vitamins, and minerals that are necessary for good health. Bees, however, do not ingest nectar/honeydew or pollen directly; instead, they cause metabolic changes in both, turning them into honey and bee bread, respectively.

Bees gather pollen from flowers, which they combine with nectar or honey and saliva that contains digestive enzymes to create bee bread. Now that flower pollen has been turned into bee pollen, it has been transported to the hive by the bee and stored in the pollen basket on its hind legs.when a combination of honey and pollen from non-flying bees is placed within the hive's cells. To shield the mixture from oxygen, wax is next added in a thin layer. The mechanism that results in the creation of bee bread is anaerobic lactic fermentation. Bee bread is improved in terms of digestion and nutrient content thanks to this kind of lacto fermentation. In general, water, protein, free amino acids, carbs, fatty acids, and other beneficial components may be found in bee bread, according to studies on its chemical makeup. Due to environmental circumstances and seasonal fluctuations, its makeup differs from one place to another. All of these circumstances make bee bread a promising functional food with unique bioactive compounds.

Chapter 1

Honeybee Life Cycle

When colonies are reproducing or when wax production is at its highest, for example, bees are at their most busy. The demand for pollen increases at these seasons, and the colony would suffer severely if there is a drop in pollen inflow (autumn and early spring) or the presence of pollen that is of poor nutritional quality. In order to meet their demands, bees are instructed to rely on their bee bread stockpile. In this review, we'll emphasize the value of bee bread for human nutrition, as well as for the well-being of the hive and the bees themselves, as well as for its abundance of bioactive compounds that have healing or preventative properties.

HYDROLOGY OF A BEES

The egg, the larva, the pupal stage, and the adult stage make up the four phases of a honey bee's life cycle.

Phase 1

Embryonic Stage:

Eggs are the beginning of every insect's life cycle, including the honey bee's. A queen creates a new colony by depositing eggs in each honeycomb cell over the winter. Unfertilized eggs develop into male honey bee drones, whereas fertilized eggs develop into female worker bees. One colony has to produce worker bees who seek for food and take care of the colony in order for it to thrive, and this requires the queen to lay fertilized eggs.

Each colony has a single queen, who mates young and produces more than five millions of sperm. A honey bee queen only makes one mating flight, during which she accumulates enough sperm to produce enough eggs to last her the rest of her life. New queens step in to take up mating and egg-laying duties when an old queen is unable to do so. Approximately half the size of a grain of rice, honey bee eggs are 1 to 1.5 mm long. Before depositing her eggs, the queen carefully inspects each cell as she makes her way through the comb. A young queen uses an orderly pattern when she lays her eggs, putting one egg adjacent to others inside a cluster. A queen can deposit up to 2,000 honey bee eggs in a single batch a cell. Queens start by depositing their eggs in the middle of the cell frame, allowing workers to put honey, royal jelly, and other larval nourishment on the outer borders. The queen, though, begins to lay less eggs in a less regular rhythm as she gets older.

An egg of a honey bee is laid by the queen, and a mucous thread ties it to the cell. The digestive system, neurological system, and external covering all develop during the initial stage of development. Larvae will emerge from the eggs after three days, and worker honey bees will feed them with honey, royal jelly, and other plant-based liquids. Legs, eyes, antennae, and wings are absent from these honey bee larvae;With a narrow mouth, they resemble rice grains. They'll eat their way up to becoming adult workers, queens, or drones.

Phase 2:
the larval stage

What Is a Larva?
When a bee emerges from its egg, it is said to be
in its larval stage. Due to the larvae's need to
ingest a lot of food quickly in order to grow, it is
a crucial stage of development.
The appearance of bee larvae
Long, white grubs without legs are the larvae of
bees. It is their responsibility to eat as much food
as they can during the larval stage so that they
can develop and go to the next stage since they
cannot leave the egg cell until they are larger.
Worker larvae or drone larvae,In the colony,
both play significant roles.

The Function of a Larva

Bee worker bees keep watch on bee larvae, who, in contrast to other insects, have extremely particular jobs to perform: Worker bees must supply enough of food to the blind larvae since they cannot see. They are unable to acquire food for themselves since they lack legs. The skin of larvae is continually lost as they grow to become adults. In order to proceed to the next phase of the bee life cycle, the larva must construct a protective shell for itself.
Larvae experience a tremendous amount of change, and they must repeatedly shed their outer skin in order to create the cocoon they will require for subsequent stages of development (pupal).

What Does Metamorphosis Mean?

The bee's growth from an egg to an adult is known as metamorphosis. The bee goes through three stages before becoming an adult, beginning as a simple egg in a honeycomb cell. The length of the bee's life depends on the caste to which it belongs; queen bees typically live the longest, although worker bees occasionally pass away after a very hectic summer.

During metamorphosis, how much larger does the larva become from its starting size?

The bee may increase in size by 1500 times from its egg stage size during the larval stage, which is a significant period of growth. As the larvae progress farther along in the bee life cycle, they consume food that is high in protein, which accounts for their quick development, Larvae experience a tremendous amount of change, and they must repeatedly shed their outer skin in order to create the cocoon they will require for subsequent stages of development (pupal).

What Does Metamorphosis Mean?

The bee's growth from an egg to an adult is known as metamorphosis. The bee goes through three stages before becoming an adult, beginning as a simple egg in a honeycomb cell. The length of the bee's life depends on the caste to which it belongs; queen bees typically live the longest, although worker bees occasionally pass away after a very hectic summer.

During metamorphosis, how much larger does the larva become from its starting size?

The bee may increase in size by 1500 times from its egg stage size during the larval stage, which is a significant period of growth. As the larvae progress farther along in the bee life cycle, they consume food that is high in protein, which accounts for their quick development.

The Larvae in the Colony Are Cared For By Who?

The duty of supplying the hive with food falls on worker bees. Worker bees are continually searching for food since an adult bee colony may number up to 80,000. Worker bees are responsible for bringing food to the colony's larvae, including lots of honey and pollen to maintain the larvae's growth. As the larvae develop into adult bees, they also take care of the upkeep of the larvae. Before the larvae mature into adult bees, worker bees can visit the developing larvae up to 10,000 times.

The Food That Larvae Eat;

- Honey and saliva: In order to dilute the honey sufficiently for the larvae, worker bees must combine the two.
- Pollen: The worker bees provide this protein-rich substance to the larvae as food.
- Royal jelly is found in lesser concentrations because the queen larvae need a high royal jelly diet.

To allow the bees to complete their whole life cycle, from eggs to adult bees in only a few short weeks, bee larvae feeds must be abundant.

What Foods Do Drone Bee Larvae Eat?

A mixture of pollen and honey, identical to the one given to worker bees, is what the larvae of drone bees eat. The only ones who receive the maximum degree of nutrients are the queens. Both the present queen bee and the future queens must be in good health in order to succeed her after she is no longer able to lay eggs. The current queen bee need a lot of nutrition in order to lay quality eggs.

Drones are made to mate with virgin queens; once they do, their purpose is fulfilled and they pass away. This is why there must be so many drone cells in a healthy colony to guarantee that there will be enough drones for upcoming mating seasons.

What Foods Are Consumed by Queen Bee Larvae?

The larvae that are specifically chosen to become future queens are given royal jelly. Pollen, chemicals from other worker bees, and proteins are all mixed together in royal jelly. Even the reproductive boosters that future queens will require are included in royal jelly. In that they consume royal jelly their entire lives, queen bees are unusual in that way.

What Are Worker Bee Larvae Feeding On?

Pollen and honey, sometimes known as "bee bread," are the primary food sources for bee larvae. The nourishment provided by this bee bread aids in the larvae's rapid development. Future queen bees consume something completely different from this diet mixture; this is for worker bees. This bee bread is full of vitamins, minerals, sugar, protein, and other nutrients that are essential for bee larvae that will develop into worker bees. All bee larvae get royal jelly for a few days, which increases their chances of surviving.

The Larval Stage of Bee Development Lasts How Long?

Bees don't spend much time as larvae, in contrast to other insects. Bees spend six days on average as larvae. Temperature, species, and environment are some of the variables that affect the length of the larval stage.

The length of the larval stage is determined by diet in what ways?

The length of the larval stage is affected by a variety of factors, including nutrition. The better the diet, the faster the larvae will grow.
Queens mature more quickly than workers or drones because better food promotes rapid growth. Simply said, they have more and better food.
The quantity of food consumed by worker bees is more, which aids in their growth, but the quality is lower than that of the queen bees. Although diet has a direct impact on how larvae develop, it is not the sole aspect in a healthy bee's life cycle.

The length of the larval stage is determined by what temperature?

Regarding the length of the larval stage, temperature has a significant impact. In general, bees are vulnerable to extreme cold. Bees in the cold take longer to develop as larvae as well as moving more slowly overall. Place the egg as usual in the cell, however the development of the egg may be slowed down by cold temperatures.

Not all types of bees congregate in hives since bees are a varied group of insects. The larval stage is still experienced by a greater number of solitary bees, but they are considerably more exposed to the environment. This indicates that they are more susceptible to extremely high or low temperatures.

How Can the Size of the Larva Be Affected by a Honeycomb Cell?

The size of the larva will differ depending on whether the eggs are deposited in a new honeycomb cell or an older, previously used honeycomb cell. Why? There is less room for the egg to develop and expand when it is placed in a honeycomb cell that has already housed other larvae.

The previous larvae lost their old skin and grew by going through multiple moults. every time you moult. Future generations are prevented from reaching their full potential because these final pieces of garbage aren't removed from the cell.

Larvae Are the Beginning of Everything

Larvae are the beginning of the process for a single bee. The bee will continue to develop until it becomes an adult, responsible for certain duties necessary for the colony's survival. Long-term colony success depends on the development of healthy larvae.

Phase 3

The third stage is known as the pupal stage, during which the little creature concealed behind the capping begins to resemble an adult bee. It ultimately grows the tiny hairs that coat its body before developing legs, eyes, and wings.

The now-adult bee exits the cell by chewing its way out after seven to fourteen days, depending on the species of bee. The queen goes through this stage first, followed by the worker bees, then the drones, and finally the worker bees again.

Phase 4

The new adult bee chews its way out of the closed-cell when it has fully developed from the pupa in stage four, the adult stage. From the egg stage until adulthood, the queen bee takes 16 days. Drone bees need 24 days to mature and take 18 to 22 days for the worker bee to reach full maturity.

Chapter 2
ANCIENT HIVES OF BEES

Ancient Egyptians maintained bees in hives that they manufactured themselves. More than 2422 BC depicts workmen blowing smoke into hives as they remove honeycombs on the walls of the Egyptian sun temple of Nyuserre Ini from the 5th Dynasty. From the 26th Dynasty (about 650 BC), inscriptions on the tomb of Pabasa depict cylindrical hives and honey contained in jars. These inscriptions also provide information on the manufacture of honey.

30 undamaged beehives that were found in the Rehov city's remains, according to archaeologist Amihai Mazar (2,000 residents in 900 BC, Israelites and Canaanites). This shows that Israel had a sophisticated honey business.

in the past, around 4,000 years. In neat rows, 150 beehives many of which were broken made of straw and unbaked clay were discovered. According to Ezra Marcus from the University of Haifa, the find offered a peek into the early beekeeping practices that have been depicted in

Near Eastern books and old artwork. The discovery of an altar next to the hives, which was adorned with fertility statues, may point to beekeeping-related religious rites. Although beekeeping has been longer than these ruins, this apiary is the oldest one that has been found. The bee colony's only protection was against the elements in traditional beehives. The bees constructed their own honeycomb within the hives because there were no interior support structures for them. As a result of many cross-attachments, the comb cannot be moved without being destroyed. To set it apart from contemporary movable-frame hives, this is frequently referred to as a fixed-frame hive. Harvest usually destroys the hives, although there have been experimental modifications employing extra top baskets that could be removed once the bees filled them with honey. These were progressively replaced by box hives of various sizes, with or without frames, and were finally replaced by more recent, contemporary machinery.

Traditional hives:

To collect honey from a traditional hive, you normally press the wax honeycomb, which involves crushing it in order to release the honey. Traditional beehives often produced more beeswax than a contemporary hive while producing significantly less honey as a result of this harvesting.
Mud hives, clay/tile hives, skeps, and bee gums are the four types of conventional beehives.

- In Egypt and Siberia, mud hives are still in use. These are lengthy cylinders constructed from a combination of unbaked mud, straw, and manure.
- In the eastern Mediterranean, keeping bees was traditionally done in clay hives or on clay tiles. In addition to ancient Egypt and the Middle East, Greece, Italy, and Malta also utilised long baked clay cylinders to some extent. They may be used individually on occasion, but were more frequently stacked in rows to offer some shade, at least for those not on top.

As they gathered honey, keepers would
smoke one end of the hive to entice the
bees to the other end.

Skeps

Over 2000 years ago, bees were kept in skeps, open-ended baskets. They were originally constructed from wicker that had been coated with mud and manure and are said to have been used for the first time in Ireland. After the Middle Ages, however, practically all of them were built of straw. Skeps were fashioned of grass or straw coils in northern and western Europe. A single entrance can be found at the base of the skep in its most basic form. The colony must create its own honeycomb, which is joined to the inside of the skep, as there is once more no internal framework given for the bees. A bushel (about 36 liters) to two pecks was the size range for early modern skeps (c. 18 litres). Skeps have two drawbacks: beekeepers are unable to check the comb for illnesses and pests, and honey removal is challenging and sometimes necessitates the eradication of the entire colony. Beekeepers either forced the bees out of the skep or attempted to make a comb with just honey in it by employing a bottom extension called an eke or a top extension called a cap in order to harvest the honey. To make the honeycomb easier to dismantle, the bees were frequently murdered, sometimes using lit sulfur. For honey extraction, skeps can also be pressed in a vice.

As of 1998, the majority of US states outlawed using skeps or any other type of hive that cannot be checked for illness and parasites.

In later skep designs, a tiny woven basket (cap) was placed on top of a small hole in the main skep. With minimal damage to the bees and their larvae, this cap served as a rudimentary super, enabling the extraction of some honey. The term "nadir," "eke," or "imp" were all used to describe this type of extension piece used in England to provide more space for brood raising. It consisted of a ring of roughly four or five coils of straw that was put below a straw beehive. Eking out a little additional space, or "eking out," more room, was done using an eke A nadir is a greater addition that was utilized when a whole tale was required below.

Old Norse skeppa, which means "basket," is where the word comes from. A "skepper," a surname that is still used in western nations, was a person who woven beehives of this type. A "girth," a ring of leather or a piece of cow horn, was used in England to regulate the thickness of straw coils, and briar strips might be used to sew the coils of straw together. Old writings, sculptures, and paintings all contain representations of skeps. A common way to identify industry on signage is using the skep ("the busy bee").

More sophisticated skeps with wooden tops that had holes over them and glass started to develop in the late 18th century the patterns would then be constructed in the glass jars, making them appealing from a commercial standpoint.

Bee gums:

Until the twentieth century, hollow tree branches were employed as building materials in the eastern United States, particularly in the southeast. Due to the fact that black gum (Nyssa sylvatica) trees frequently provided these "gums," the term "gums" was used.
In apiaries or "bee yards," pieces of the hollow trees were placed upright. In order to provide a connection for the honeycomb, sticks or crossed sticks were occasionally inserted beneath a board cover. Similar to skeps, this colony was wiped off by the honey harvest. The bees were frequently killed by the harvester before their nest could even be accessed. A metal cylinder filled with burning sulfur was inserted into the hole to accomplish this In the past, beekeepers in Central Europe employed both natural tree hollows and man-madely hollowed tree trunks extensively. Such a hive was shielded from predators and inclement weather (rain, cold, etc.) in various ways in Poland, where it was known as a "bar" (woodpeckers, bears, pine martens,

forest dormice). Only a little piece of wood was removed to serve as protection from the aperture, and smoke was used to momentarily calm the bees, preventing the colony from being destroyed when honey was harvested from them. Bee gums' continued usage is partly due to the fact that it enables honey producers to set themselves apart from rivals and command greater prices for their wares honey. Despite being known as log hives in Europe, Mont-Lozère, France, is one location where bee gums are still utilized. These log hives are hollowed out artificially and are chopped to a particular size, making them shorter than bee gums in length.

Modern hives:

Although they were refined from early stages of development produced in the 18th century, the earliest recognizable modern beehive designs emerged in the 19th century.
Thomas Wildman, who reported improvements over the harmful old skep-based beekeeping so that the bees would not need to be killed in order to extract the honey, documented intermediate phases in hive construction in the years 1768–1770, for instance. For instance, Wildman fastened a parallel row of hardwood bars across the top of a straw hive or skep (with a separate straw top to be fixed on later) "so that there are in all seven bars of deal" [in a 10-inch-diameter (250 mm) hive] "to which the bees fix their combs]. Additionally, he provided a description He described using these hives in a multi-story configuration, foreshadowing the modern use of supers: he described adding (at the proper time) successive straw hives below, and eventually removing the ones above when free of brood and filled with honey, so that the bees could be

preserved separately at the harvest for the following season. In addition, Wildman foreshadowed more contemporary applications of movable-comb hives by describing a further development that involved employing hives with "slide frames" for the bees to construct their comb. In addition to providing a detailed translation of Reaumur's description of the natural history of bees, Wildman acknowledged the contributions made to our understanding of bees by Swammerdam, Maraldi, and de Reaumur. He also explained the many types of bees that exist today mentioning, in particular, tales from Brittany from the 1750s, attributed to Comte de la Bourdonnaye, the efforts of others in creating hives for the protection of bee-life when taking the crop.

Vertical or horizontal hives are both possible. Three primary types of contemporary hives are in widespread usage around the globe:

- atop-bar hive
- either the Langstroth hive
- the Warre hive

For Apis mellifera and Apis cerana, most hives have been modified. Other hives have been created and enhanced for certain meliponines, including Melipona beecheii. Such hives include the UTOB hive and the Nogueira Neto hive, for instance.

Vertical hives

The Rev. Lorenzo Langstroth, who copyrighted
his design in the United States on October 5,
1852, gave the name Langstroth hives to vertical
hives. The concepts of Johann Dzierzon and
other pioneers in apiculture served as the
foundation for it. The utilization of hanging
frames, bee gaps between them and other
elements, and a top-worked hive are all
combined in this arrangement. Many beekeepers
across the world, both professional and amateur,
now use variations of his design as the standard
kind of hive. To increase the amount of room the
bees may use, Langstroth hive bodies can be
stacked. Although several materials may be used
to make them, wood is the most frequent. What
makes up a Langstroth hive today?

- This bottom board features a bee entrance.
- the lowest box is where the queen lays her
  eggs, and the boxes above are where the
  honey is kept.
- Weather-proofing features include the
  inside cover and top cap.

Single Long Box

Single, long boxes with parallel-hanging bars are referred to as horizontal hives. A typical form of horizontal hive has a body that resembles an inverted trapezoid often, although it can also have a rectangular cross-section and support standard frames. They employ the notion of bee space and feature moveable comb. They were created as an affordable replacement for the typical Langstroth hives and machinery. In order to check or work on the hive, they don't require the beekeeper to raise bulky supers. They are well-liked in the US as a result of their compatibility with the organic, drug-free ideologies of many of the country's new beekeeping enthusiasts. Initial investment expenditures and necessary equipment are often a lot less than other hive designs. The best hives are frequently constructed from scrap wood. Beekeepers may do all checks and manipulations while lifting just one comb at a time and bending minimally with horizontal hives; they are not required to raise super boxes. Single-box hives could be hanged out of the way in regions where large terrestrial animals like bears and honey badgers pose a hazard to beehives. In other places, they are frequently elevated so that the beekeeper may comfortably check and work on them.

The disadvantages of this method include the fact that most honey extractors cannot spin unsupported combs, and if more room is needed for honey storage, it is typically not viable to enlarge the hive. almost all horizontal hives is difficult for one person to lift and carry.

Instead of frames, top-bars are frequently used in horizontal hives. Top bars don't require buying or assembling frames; they are simply basic lengths of wood that are frequently manufactured by cutting waste wood to size. Contrary to typical frames, which allow a bee-space gap so that the bees may travel up and down between hive boxes, the top bars create a continuous roof over the hive chamber. In most cases, the beekeeper simply gives the bees a little bit of foundation wax to start with, or none at all. In order for the comb to hang on the top bar, the bees create it. In a natural hole, bees create wax in a manner consistent with nature. Honey is often extracted by crushing and straining rather than centrifuging as an unsupported comb made from a top bar is typically unable to be centrifuged in a honey extractor. A top-bar hive produces a harvest of beeswax in addition to honey because the bees need to rebuild their comb once the honey is gathered. To completely keep the brood regions and the honey apart, queen excluders may or may not be utilized. Honey may still be gathered without harming bees or brood even if no queen excluder is employed since bees store the majority of their honey in locations apart from where they are rearing the brood.

- Modified top bar for the cathedral hive. A half-hexagon is created by slicing the top bar into three equal pieces and joining them at 120° angles.

The long box hive

The long box hive is a one-story structure that works like top-bar hives from Kenya and Tanzania by working horizontally with fully covered frames. In the Southeast of the United States, this non-stacked form was more widely used a century ago, but it eventually lost favor due to its impracticality for transport. The long box hive is being used again, albeit sparingly, as a result of the recent craze for horizontal top-bar hives. You can also call it "long hive," "new concept hive," "single storey hive," or "Poppleton hive."

Variations

- Uses 32 conventional Langstroth deep frames without any supers for the long Langstroth hive.
- Long-deep (DLD) hive at Dartington The DLD, which was created by mounting two Deep National hives side by side, has a maximum frame capacity of 21 at 360 by 300 millimeters (14 in. 12 in. There is a chance that the brood box will include two colonies, such as a "swarm" and a "parent," which will be divided by a loose Divider.Board, as both ends have entrances. It contains half-size honey supers that use six frames, weigh less than full supers, and are thus simpler to lift than 12-frame National supers. In order to maintain bees on his London roofs, Robin Dartington first created the Dartington.
- The Dartington Long Deep was the basis for the 2009 debut of the Beehaus Hive, a unique beehive design. A top-bar hive and a Langstroth hive have combined to create it.

- By Georges de Layens in 1864, he created the Layens Hive. In Romania and Spain, this hive is a well-liked standard. When forced industrialization standardized all apiaries in the early 1900s, it was also well-liked in Russia.

Chapter 3
HONEY BREAD

Free amino acids: Bee Bread Composition 1
The amount of free amino acids in bee bread has been studied in several research. In two research by Mohammad et al. and Othman et al., for instance, Malaysian bee bread was examined. Four multifloral bee breads were examined using chromatographic separation in the first study; the samples came from the following plants: Mimosa pudica, Sphagneticola trilobata, Bidens pilosa, Cassia sp, Areca Citrus, catechu, Cassia siamea, Peltophorum pterocarpum, Phaleria capitata, aurantifolia, and Ageratum conyzoides. The WatersAccQ Tag technique was used in the second investigation to examine three samples. The findings from the two research projects demonstrated the phenylalanine, valine, histidine, methionine, isoleucine, leucine, threonine, alanine, arginine, tyrosine, glycine, proline, hydroxyproline, serine, glutamic acid, aspartic acid, and lysine were found in samples of bee bread.

Additionally, Trifolium, Impatiens, Rubus, Acer, Cirsium, Euscaphis, Cryptotaenia, Glycine, Coriandrum, Rosa, Prunus, Taraxacum, Camelina, Ranunculus, Salix, and Andira were investigated, along with 51 other English bee bread samples. These samples contained a variety of amino acids, including aspartate, glutamate, asparagine, serine, glutamine, histidine, glycine, threonine, arginine, alanine, -aminobutyric acid, tyrosine, cysteine, valine, methionine, tryptophan, phenylalanine, isoleucine, leucine, lysine, and pro using gas chromatography mass The amino acids alanine, aspartic acid, glutamine, serine, leucine, isoleucine, methionine, threonine, valine, tryptophan, cysteine, phenylalanine, and proline were all present in the two American samples examined by DeGrandi-Hoffman et al. via spectrometry (GC-MS) analysis. Additionally, Bayram et al. [analyzed five samples of Turkish bee bread and discovered the following amino acids: tryptophan, taurine, l-tyrosine, l-phenylalanine, l-isoleucine, l-leucine, gamma-aminobutyric acid, 3-amino isobutyric acid, l-methionine, l-2-aminoadipic acid, beta-alan l-alanine, l-threonine, l-serine, l-glycine, l-asparagine, l-glutamine, l-proline, sarcosine, l-arginine, l-cystine, these amino acids: histidine, l-ornithine, l-carnosine, l-lysine, and l-anserine. diverse bee breads from throughout the world's chemical makeup.

Generally speaking, both floral (nectar, honeydew, and primary pollen) and animal (bee secretions) sources are credited with the amino acids found in bee bread. Since pollen is the primary source, some bee products, such bee pollen, honey, and bee bread, may need to be classified botanically based on their amino acid composition or other features. Tryptophan, for example, is regarded as a prospective biomarker for acacia-related bee products, and arginine is a marker for chestnut-based hive products. The amino acids included in bee bread have been shown to be crucial not only for the authentication of bee goods but also for a variety of other functions. bodily functions that are physiological. Methionine, an essential amino acid, participates in the DNA methylation reaction, protein synthesis, glutathione (GSH) precursor function, and acts as a powerful antioxidant agent by removing excess reactive oxygen species (ROS), protecting tissues from oxidative stress. It is also present in high amounts in functional foods, including bee products. In addition to having essential gluconeogenic properties, arginine also has immunomodulatory properties that can improve the functioning of macrophages and T cells (CD8+) and T cells. In order to provide a beneficial nutraceutical dietary supplement, bee bread must be incorporated into the everyday diet of people.

Sugars

The energy needed for bees to survive is produced from carbohydrates. On the amount of sugar in bee bread, several research have been done. For instance, the daily energy requirements of bee workers are around 4 mg of sugar [3,19]. High-performance liquid chromatography with refractive index detection (HPLC-RID) was used to analyze a Moroccan multifloral sample to estimate the amount of free sugar in bee bread (Bupleurum spinosum, Anethum Anacyclus, Graveolens, Calendula officinalis, Quercus ilex, Eucalyptus, and Punica granatum, and Acacia). Following glucose (5.7 0.4 g/100 g), fructose (11.8 0.6 g/100 g), and a trace quantity of trehalose (0.92 0.01 g/100 g), according to the data, was the principal representative sugar. Dranca et al. [reported that Romanian bee bread includes There are just little amounts of melezitose and raffinose (0.97 g/100 g and 0.96 g/100 g, respectively) and 19.73 g/100 g of fructose and 8.82 g/100 g of glucose. Additionally, the results of Urcan et al. [22] for five multifloral bee bread samples (Brassicaceae,

Poaceae, Myrtaceae, Rutaceae, Asteraceae, Fabaceae, Tiliaceae, Fabaceae, Rosaceae, Plantaginaceae, Fabaceae, Asteraceae, Lamiaceae, Salicaceae, Rosaceae, and F 0.56 0.02 g/100 g to 0.87 0.01 g/100 g, respectively). Contrarily, in a study by Mohammad et al., a sugar profile showed that glucose was the main free sugar present in four Malaysian multifloral bee breads analyzed by HPLC coupled with an evaporative light scattering detector (ELSD); the values ranged between 10.270 0.140 g/100 g and 12.397 0.980 g/100 g.

After fructose, which ranged from 0.396 0.000 to 1.488 0.140 g/100 g, and maltose, which ranged from 0.694 0.140 to 1.994 0.000 g/100 g, sucrose had the second-highest sugar concentration (Table 1). There are several variables that might account for this considerable diversity, including the time of harvest, the type of plants used, and using lactic acid bacteria to break down carbohydrates.

Oleic Acids

One of the most vital components of bee bread is fatty acids. Bakour et al. analyzed Moroccan bee bread using gas chromatography combined with flame ionization detection (GC-FID), and they were able to identify and quantify fourteen saturated and eleven unsaturated fatty acids, with -linolenic and arachidonic acid having the highest levels at 25 1% and 23.2 0.5%, respectively. However, Kaplan et alinvestigation .'s of Turkish bee bread using GC-MS and GC-FID in two experiments revealed that in eight monofloral samples in the first research and five monofloral samples in the second study, a total of seventeen saturated fatty acids and twenty unsaturated fatty acids had been found. Recently, Dranca and colleagues presented a research in which the Romanian bee bread's GC-MS study revealed that it contained 37 fatty acids, with 76.87% of them being unsaturated and 23.13% of them being saturated. Considering the results of the earlier studies, it is clear that the individual fatty acids present in different bee breads are the same; however, the

concentrations of these fatty acids can differ
depending on the geo-climatic factors, the origin
of the pollen flowers, or even between members
of the same species at the same growth site.

Minerals

Soil minerals are absorbed by plants through their roots, while bees use nectar, honeydew, and pollen from flowers to make their bread. According to macro- and microelement content, bee bread is one of the richest hive products. In their study of Moroccan bee bread, Bakour et al. found that potassium (338 8 mg/100 g) was the most abundant mineral, followed by phosphorus (251 4 mg/100 g), calcium (198 4 mg/100 g), magnesium (61 2 mg/100 g), iron (27.3 0.3 mg/100 g), sodium (14.2 0.1 mg/100 g), zinc (3.31 0.04 mg/100 Depending on the mineral composition of the honey bread Agroclimatic factors, particular mellifera species, a plant's growing location, and the harvesting season. The concentration and mineral makeup of bee bread might also be impacted by the techniques utilized for sample collection and conditioning storage.

Potassium (6524.9 610.6 mg/kg), phosphorus (6402.28 163.29 mg/kg), and magnesium (1635.4 215.4 mg/kg) were the three minerals with the highest concentrations in Malaysian bee bread.

In a similar vein, Eleazu et al. discovered significant quantities of calcium, phosphorus, potassium, magnesium, iron, zinc, and manganese in Malaysian bee bread. Aside from that, the ICP-MS analysis of samples of Serbian bee bread revealed their high levels of sodium, magnesium, potassium, calcium, manganese, selenium, zinc, and copper. Calcium, magnesium, and potassium were the three minerals that were most prevalent.
In numerous biochemical and physiological processes that occur in humans, minerals play an important role. For instance, a diet high in potassium, an oligoelement that exhibits strongly in samples of bee bread from various floral and geographic origins, can lower blood pressure and prevent cardiovascular disorders in both human and animal models. The human body contains phosphorus, the sixth-most common metal, in intimately linked to the production of nucleic acids, the activity of enzymes, the use of

energy and lipids, the contraction of skeletal and non-skeletal muscles, and bone mineralization. The cofactors of several antioxidant and non-antioxidant enzymes are micro-elements, such as antioxidant minerals including zinc, iron, manganese, selenium, and copper. They function well in maintaining the integrity of the human body's metabolism.

The organic acids

In addition to being utilized as food preservatives, organic acids are what provide bee products their microbiological and digestive qualities. The amount of knowledge on the organic acid content of bee bread that is now accessible in the literature is still rather small. Gluconic acid (79.2 g/kg), formic acid (6.75 g/kg), acetic acid (10.7 g/kg), propionic acid (1.3 g/kg), and butyric acid (0.33 g/kg) were all detected in a recent research by Dranca et alHPLC-DAD .'s analysis of Romanian bee bread. Oxalic acid was the sole organic acid discovered in the Moroccan bee bread that Bakour et al. examined. In bee bread, there are organic acids. vary according on the source of the botanical (age, species, and vegetable tissue). The organic acid content of bee bread may be compared to that of bee pollen because it is a product made from bee pollen. Six multifloral and four monofloral bee pollen samples from different parts of Turkey were analyzed by Kalaycioglu and colleagues. They found that the most quantified organic acids were gluconic acid (5.9-32 g/kg), lactic acid (0.72-1.2 g/kg), tartaric acid (0.17-0.30 g/kg), succinic acid (0.092-0.40 g/kg), and citric acid (0.19-0.31 g Gluconoic acid is a The primary organic acid in bee bread had strong antibacterial effects against anaerobic (Porphyromonas gingivalis), gram-negative (Escherichia coli), and gram-positive (Staphylococcus aureus) bacteria. It also successfully penetrated biofilms. Gluconic acid and polymyxin B together demonstrated strong antibacterial activity and excellent biofilm penetration. A further beneficial component of bee products called acetic acid has been shown to have anti-fungal properties against the toxic mold Aspergillus flavus. As a result, bee bread extracts hold potential as natural food preservatives and antibiotics.

Vitamins

Organic molecules known as vitamins have a variety of biochemical roles in development, the control of mineral metabolism, and cell differentiation. Some vitamins also have antioxidant action, while others act as precursors to enzyme cofactors. The research indicates that the amount of vitamins in bee bread depends significantly on the type of plant it is made from. In a comparison of the vitamin contents of bee pollen and bee bread samples from the same plant source (Prunus dulcis) after seven, twenty-one, and forty-two days, Loper et al. discovered that pollen from the flowers continued to lose vitamin content over the forty-two day storage period. The nutritional content of bee bread hasn't received much research up to this point.

Content of Polyphenols

A number of bioactive components in bee bread from various geographical origins have been discovered thanks to the development of sophisticated techniques for the separation and purification of molecules, such such as GC and HPLC (high-performance liquid chromatography),HPLC), as well as other identification techniques, such as mass spectroscopy (MS), thin-layer chromatography (TLC), and other combined techniques.

Plants respond to a variety of biotic and abiotic stress situations by producing polyphenol chemicals as secondary metabolites. These chemicals may be split into two categories: hydrophilic antioxidants, such vitamin C and phenolic acids, and lipophilic antioxidants, including carotenoids, tocopherols, and flavonoids. Considering its high Its bioactivities are caused by the antioxidants in bee bread. For instance, Oltica and colleagues discovered a strong correlation between antioxidant content (polyphenols, flavonols, flavones, and flavanones) and antioxidant activity as measured by the 2,2-diphenyl-1-picrylhydrazyl (DPPH), trolox equivalent antioxidant capacity (TEAC), and ferric reducing antioxidant power (FRAP) tests, which explains their contribution to the antioxidant effects of bee bread extracts. It is well knowledge that the phytochemical content of functional foods, including extracts from bee products, is greatly influenced by the kind of soil, the geographic location, and the variety of plants. Additionally, the amount and selectivity of the extract components are influenced by the solvent and extraction technique utilized. The content of bees' chemicals has been shown to vary. diverse floral and geographic bread extracts.

Microorganisms

In order to enhance bee bread with freshly created nutrients, various microorganisms, including bacteria and fungus, are used throughout the preparation process. Bees' saliva, which is added to pollen as the basic material for bee bread, is where the microbes present in bee bread are believed to have originated. The health of adult bees and the sustenance of larvae are both critically dependent on this microbiome, which also enhances the nutritional value of various substances and facilitates the digestion of carbohydrates. Bee bread can also have the qualities of a probiotic food due to its high microbial content. The following fungus composition in bee bread was shown by a study by Dimov et al. Ascosphaera, Alternaria, Monilinia, Sclerotinia, Penicillium,

Enzymes

Amylase, invertase, phosphatases, transferases, and glucose oxidase are among the enzymes found in high concentrations in bee bread, and they are all crucial. To finish the maturation process of the honey, the bees add invertase and glucose oxidase, which are mostly generated in the hypopharyngeal glands. On the other hand, certain enzymes, including catalase and phosphatase, come from nectar, honeydew, or pollen. Additionally, bee bread contains enzyme cofactors such biotin, glutathione, and NAD. These enzymes are capable of converting molecules with high molecular weight into proteins and polysaccharides, two examples of molecules with low molecular weight. Bee pollen is less digestible as a result, making bee bread more so.

Bee bread has antioxidant properties, which has a bioactive effect.

One of the most crucial components of bee bread is antioxidant molecules, as was already discussed. Using spectrophotometric methods, a number of studies have assessed these compounds' antioxidant potential. Different Malaysian bee bread extracts were put through DPPH, ABTS, and FRAP experiments to determine their antioxidant capabilities. Akhir et al. and Othman et al (hexanoic, ethanolic, and distilled water extracts). The solvents utilized had an impact on the bee bread's bioactivity, the authors demonstrated. The ethanolic extract, which was subsequently followed by the hexanoic and aqueous extracts in order of potency, was the strongest extract. Zuluaga et al. similarly assessed the antioxidant activity of 15 samples of Colombian bee bread. According to the authors, each extract demonstrated strong antioxidant properties activity. When tested for FRAP and antioxidant activity, the scientists found that all of the extracts had favorable results. TEAC techniques; their total flavonoid concentration varied from 1.9 to 4.5 mg equivalent of quercetin/g, while their total phenolic content varied from 2.5 to 13.7 mg equivalent of gallic acid/g.

Through the use of three different extraction solvents, Bakour et al. examined the antioxidant activity of Moroccan bee bread in three trials (ethanol, ethyl acetate, and methanol).
According to the findings, the ethanolic extract had the lowest recorded values of IC50/EC5050 for the antioxidant activity measured by the three tests—DPPH, ABTS, and reducing power—followed by the methanolic and ethyl acetate extracts.
The ability of European bee bread to act as an antioxidant in vitro was established by several research published between 2004 and 2020. The findings indicated. that all of the samples were tested have strong antioxidant activity.

Effect of Bee Bread on Tumours

Two investigations, the first of which was conducted by Markiewicz-ukowska et al., examined the anticancer efficacy of bee bread in vitro. The viability of the glioblastoma cell line (U87MG) after 24 hours, 48 hours, and 72 hours was examined in this study using various ethanolic extracts of bee bread samples obtained from Poland. The findings demonstrated that the viability of cancer cells was decreased by 49% to 66% by the bee bread ethanolic extract. Mostly after 72 hours of interaction, this inhibitory impact became apparent.

The second research was conducted by Sobral et al., who assessed the anticancer efficacy of bee bread from northern Portugal against various NCI-H460 (non-cellular lung cancer), HepG2, HeLa, MCF-7 (breast adenocarcinoma), and non-tumor liver cells are examples of human tumor cell lines (porcine liver cells, PLP2). None of the bee bread samples was lethal to normal cells, although they did exhibit low to moderate cytotoxicity, with concentrations ranging from >400 to 68 g/mL.

Effect on Blood Pressure

Nagai et al. used bee bread enzymatic hydrolysates produced by three proteases, including pepsin, trypsin, and papain, to assess the hypotensive impact of bee bread. The pepsin hydrolyzate, trypsin hydrolyzate, and papain hydrolyzate all shown inhibitory activity for the angiotensin I converting enzyme of 1.48 mg protein/mL, 2.16 mg protein/mL, and 5.41 mg protein/mL, respectively.

Enzymes that Hydrolyze Carbohydrates Have an Inhibitory Effect

The development of novel drugs with a high potential for inhibiting carbohydrate-hydrolyzing enzymes is only one example of how the first line of treatment strategy must be controlled in order to effectively manage diabetes. Alpha-amylase may be inhibited by bee bread methanolic extract, with an IC50% of 3.57 mg/mL, according to in vitro research. It has been shown via the use of molecular docking, UV absorption, and fluorescence quenching studies that bee bread includes functional fatty acids that engage with the amino acid residues of hydrolyzing enzymes through hydrogen bonds and van der Waals interactions. The product bee bread is sophisticated and has a high Flavonoid content; flavonoids are recognized for their ability to bind to the active site of an enzyme through bond and alkyl interactions, which are assisted by the various methyl and hydroxyl groups that make up the flavonoid's structure. In vivo research on the pharmacological effects of bee bread has demonstrated that it can regulate metabolic abnormalities by inhibiting carbohydrate-hydrolyzing enzymes.

Bee Bread's Beneficial Microorganisms

Probiotics are described by the Food and Agriculture Organization and the World Health Organization as "live bacteria that when provided in suitable proportions bestow a health benefit on the host." Human probiotic strains are usually found in the genera Lactobacilli, Bifidobacteria lactococcus, Streptococcus, and Enterococcus, as well as a few yeast strains from the species Saccharomyces.

Due to its positive effects in the treatment of a number of human ailments, including inflammatory bowel disorders, gut infections, allergies, asthma, pulmonary infections, and even mental conditions, probiotic research has recently attracted significant scientific and popular attention. Probiotics' immunomodulatory impact, according to a new study, may be helpful in the context of COVID-19 infection. Given the fact that there is a strong link between probiotic bacteria and human health, consumers are growing increasingly aware about this relationship and demanding more functional foods, particularly fermented foods and drinks, in their diets.

The probiotic qualities of the bee bread's

microbial makeup provide it intriguing
medicinal advantages. In their review research,
Khalifa et al. hypothesized that the cholesterol-
lowering substances produced by Lactobacillus
bacteria in bee bread contribute to its
extraordinary hypolipidemic impact.
Additionally, the presence of fructophilic lactic
acid and lactobacillus bacteria in bee bread
offers a promising source of chemicals with high
techno-functional properties that are used in the
food industry as a food preservative or in
functional cultures for the industrial production
of fermented foods.

Bee Bread's antimicrobial properties

Abouda et al. tested the antibacterial efficacy of bee bread from different locations of Morocco against the germs Staphylococcus aureus, Bacillus cereus, Pseudomonas aeruginosa, and Escherichia coli. All of the bee bread samples had excellent antibacterial activity against the bacterial strains, with greater susceptibility to Gram-positive bacteria than Gram-negative bacteria, according to the data.

Against Staphylococcus aureus and Staphylococcus epidermidis, four types of bee bread were evaluated by Baltruaityt et al. The bee bread samples demonstrated non-peroxide antibacterial activity, according to the findings after the product was neutralized and treated with catalase. Similarly, Ivaniov et al. demonstrated that samples of bee bread from five areas of Ukraine have antibacterial activity against four bacterial strains, including two Gram-positive (Bacillus thuringiensis and Staphylococcus aureus) and two Gram-negative

(Bacillus spp. E. Gram-negative bacteria like E. coli and Salmonella enterica both exist. According to the results, the minimum inhibitory concentrations ranged between 6.40 g mL-1 and 25.58 g mL-1.

The hydromethanolic extract of Moroccan multifloral bee bread was tested against six bacterial strains, including Bacillus cereus, Staphylococcus aureus, Escherichia coli, Enterobacter cloacae, Salmonella typhimurium, and Listeria monocytogenes. It was discovered that the minimum inhibitory concentration (MIC) and minimum bactericidal concentration (MBC) values ranged between 0.04 mg/mL and 0.25 In addition to Aspergillus fumigatus, Aspergillus ochraceus, Aspergillus niger, and Aspergillus niger, the bee bread sample was also efficient against Penicillium ochrochloron, Penicillium verrucosum, and Penicillium funiculosum var. cyclopium. The MIC and MBC values were 0.35 to 1 mg/mL and 0.70 to 1.40 mg/mL, respectively, in the obtained ranges.

The properties of bee bread that are antiviral and antimicrobial.

According to a research by Didaras et al., Greek bee bread's aqueous extract was effective against both Gram-positive and Gram-negative bacteria, with MIC values between 3.9 and 48 mg/mL and 7.8 and 90.4 mg/mL, respectively, for Gram-positive bacteria. Bee bread ethanolic extracts (70%, 95%, 80%, and 50%) have also been demonstrated to exhibit potent antibiotic action against Gram-positive bacteria (Bacillus cereus, Clostridium perfringens,

Listeria monocytogene, methicillin-resistant Staphylococcus aureus, Staphylococcus epidermidis, Bacillus subtilis, Salmonella enterica, Escherichia coli, Shigella, and Pseudomonas aeruginosa, as well as Gram-negative bacteria (Haemophilus influenza, Klebsiella pneumonia, Salmonella enterica, Escherichia coli, Shigella, and (Candida albicans, Aspergillus niger, Candida glabrata, Candida tropicalis, Aspergillus clavatus, Aspergillus flavus, Aspergillus versicolor,

Penicillium expansum, Penicillium chrysogenum, and Penicillium griseofulvum). Generally speaking, it appears from research that Gram-positive bacteria are more vulnerable to bee bread extract than Gram-negative bacteria. This might be as a result of Gram-negative bacteria having a cytoplasmic membrane that includes less anionic phospholipids than Gram-positive bacteria. Some Gram-negative bacteria are resistant to antibiotics due to this unique makeup of the bacterium.

Only Didaras et alstudy .'s against the EV-D68 virus did research on the antiviral properties of bee bread up until this point. IC50 values of 0.048 to 5.45 mg/mL and CC50 values of 0.17 to 8.60 mg/mL were found in the findings, which were encouraging. Numerous studies have hypothesized that the polyphenol content of bee products, including caffeic acid, chrysin, galangin, and rutin, is what gives them their antiviral properties [91,92]. Flavonoids may prevent SARS, according to recent in silico research.

Antimicrobial Action Mechanisms That Have Been Proposed

A lot of people are interested in learning more about developing novel, safer, and more potent antibacterial compounds from food and food byproducts. several scientists globally. Due to their hydroxyl groups (OH), phenolic compounds and certain antioxidant molecules interact with the bacterial cell membrane through hydrogen bonding, leading to two potential coupled processes for how they exert their antibacterial effects. The first process involves the destruction of the bacterial membrane's structure, which results in the expulsion of the cell's contents. The second process relies on the delocalization of electrons, which causes the cell membrane to become depolarized and the pH gradient across the membrane to decrease, resulting in a decrease in ATP production [96]. The relative location of each antioxidant molecule's hydroxyl group on its phenolic nucleus has a significant impact on the antibacterial activity of phenolic compounds.

Numerous beneficial compounds with strong antibacterial activity may be found in bee bread. Several Studies have demonstrated that flavonoids cause their antibacterial effects by focusing on a variety of pathways and mechanisms, including the inhibition of nucleic acid synthesis, the disruption of cytoplasmic membrane function, the modification of cell membrane permeability, and the interaction with some crucial bacterial enzymes. According to a recent study by Wang and colleagues, quercetin, a common flavonol, kills bacteria like Escherichia coli and Staphylococcus aureus by disrupting their cell walls and membrane structures and by preventing the production of new proteins. Quercetin also inhibits DNA synthesis and bacterial energy consumption. Kaempferol, a flavonol substance often found in bee bread, has been demonstrated to inhibit DNA PriA helicase and reduce ATPase activity in Staphylococcus aureus, indicating the possibility of using it as a natural component in the creation of fresh, effective antibiotics for this organism. Other flavonoids, such apigenin, have also been studied to see if they have any antibacterial properties. Apigenin is said to prevent Staphylococcus aureus from producing RNA polymerase and DNA gyrase.

It has been shown that organic acids (aromatic and aliphatic) also exhibit bacteriostatic and bactericidal properties in addition to phenolic chemicals. The bacterial membrane is easily penetrated by organic acids, which, once within the cells, release protons (H+), lowering intracellular pH, damaging macromolecules, and weakening bacterial walls. Individual organic acids including gluconic, acetic, and formic acids have been extensively studied for their antibacterial characteristics. many scientists. In one study, it was demonstrated that the main organic acid in bee bread, gluconic acid, depolarized membrane cells and interfered with the integrity of membranes. The elongation factors TU and GOS, the polymerase alpha subunit, C-acetyltransferase 1OS, and chaperone proteins are among the genes whose expression is sabotaged by acetic acid, according to a recent research. The germination of Conidia and the generation of aflatoxin were both significantly inhibited by acetic acid in addition to its antibacterial effects. The interaction between bee bread extracts' active components and microbial cells through one or more separate modes of action may also contribute to the antibacterial activity of the extracts. Bee bread may be beneficial, according to recent study used as a potential antibacterial and natural food preservation component.

The bioactive compounds included in bee bread may have antimicrobial effects.
Moroccan bee bread was administered orally for 15 days at a dose of 100 mg/kg to Wistar rats with type 1 diabetes to assess its pharmacological effects. The sample was extracted using ethyl acetate. The outcomes demonstrated that the bee bread was successful in lowering blood glucose levels, protected against weight loss brought on by diabetes, had a hypolipidemic impact, and shielded diabetic rats from a rise in the coronary risk index, atherogenic index, and cardiovascular index.

Bakour et al. further assessed the titanium toxicity of the same sample's ethanolic extract. Titanium dioxide nanoparticles were tested in Wistar rats for toxicity. According to the findings, bee bread significantly protected against a drop in albumin and total protein levels while lowering the levels of aspartate aminotransferase (AST), alanine aminotransferase (ALT), lactate dehydrogenase (LDH), blood glucose, sodium, potassium, and chloride. Bee bread also decreased the biochemical changes brought on by aluminum in rats at doses of 500 and 750 mg/kg by increasing hematocrit, hemoglobin, red blood cells, mean corpuscular hemoglobin (MCH), mean corpuscular volume (MCV), mean corpuscular hemoglobin concentration (MCHC), urine sodium, and creatinine clearance, and decreasing platelets, monocytes, lymphocytes, leukocytes, ALT, AST, C-reactive protein (CR

Bee bread's pharmacological characteristics.

In two trials, rats fed a high-fat diet to make them obese were tested with Malaysian bee bread; the dose in both cases was 0.5 g/kg administered orally with distilled water. In the first study, Eleazu et al. found that the administration of bee bread to obese rats decreased the percentage change in body weight, BMI index, kidney weight, MDA concentrations, inflammatory cells in kidney tissue, NFkB, TNF-, interleukin-l-beta, and Bax, while increasing the levels of SOD, GPx, GST, and TAA, and decreasing the Bowman's capsule space in the urinary chambers of the kidneys. Bee bread was given to obese male Sprague-Dawley rats to enhance their lipid profile in the second trial by Othman et al It demonstrated its capacity to increase nitric oxide release, promote endothelial nitric oxide synthase (eNOS), and promote cyclic guanosine monophosphate (cGMP) immunoexpression, and it inhibited the activity of vasorelaxation in response to aortic inflammatory markers and their impaired vasorelaxation. Suleiman et al. employed the same procedure for high-fat diet-induced obese rats to investigate the preventive effects of bee bread at a dose of 0.5 g/kg once daily for 12 weeks on testicular oxidative stress, inflammation, apoptosis, and lactate transport in the testes of obese rats.

In the same vein, Martiniakova et al. showed that oral treatment of monofloral bee bread extract (Brassica napus L.) dramatically reduced blood glucose levels, avoided lipid abnormalities, and negatively affected the bone shape of Zucker diabetic fatty rats. The impact of dietary changes was also demonstrated by Hak et al on the chemistry of the meat of Japanese quails when bee bread powder is used. Bee bread changed the proportions of water, crude protein, fat, and cholesterol in the fowl breast muscle while increasing the amounts of water, fat, and cholesterol in the quail thigh muscle.

By administering two doses of bee bread orally to adult female Sprague-Dawley rats, Doanyiit et al. in Turkey investigated the impact of bee

bread on leptin and ghrelin expression in obese
rats. The findings revealed that bee bread
increased leptin immunoreactivity, decreased
ghrelin immunoreactivity, and decreased the
number of apoptotic cells in the hypothalamus
and MDA levels. Moreover, it was demonstrated
that Slovakian bee bread enhanced femoral bone
structure and decreased femoral bone density
Zucker diabetic fatty rats' glucose and lipid
metabolism was also studied, as was the ability
of Chinese bee bread to control lipid
metabolism.

Clinical Studies Using Bee Bread
Hepatitis-Preventive Effect

Patients with chronic hepatitis were used in eksteryt et alstudy .'s of bee bread. The most crucial clinically significant finding was a marked improvement in blood parameters, such as erythrocyte count, hemoglobin, leukocytes, C-reactive protein (CRP), blood sugar, aspartate aminotransferase (AST), alanine aminotransferase (ALT), and bilirubin

Effect of preventing atherogenic dyslipidemia

Using a combination of honey, pollen, and bee bread, Kas'ianenko et al. assessed the efficacy of treating individuals with atherogenic dyslipidemia. In 157 individuals (64 men and 93 women) between the ages of 39 and 72, the markers of atherogenic dyslipidemia were assessed. There were four groups created from these patients:
(1) treated with honey and pollen,
 (2) treated with bee bread alone,

(3) treated with a lipid-lowering diet alone,
 (4) treated with a lipid-lowering diet and just honey or pollen,
 (5) treated with a lipid-lowering diet and alone. The findings demonstrated a substantial lipid-lowering impact in patients ingesting pollen and honey (total cholesterol fell by 18.3% and LDL-C decreased by 23.9%), as well as bee bread (total cholesterol decreased by 15.7% and LDL-C decreased by 20.5%).

Improvement of Visual Acuity

In 34 youngsters (aged 6 to 17) with thyroid illness who were ingesting bee bread, Jaruaitien et al. looked at refractive status, visual acuity, and ocular prophylaxis before and after. As a result of using bee bread, the individuals in this study had improved visual acuity.

Improved athletic performance and ergogenic effect

The impact of supplementing with bee bread during recovering on athletic performance was investigated by Chen et al. For the investigation, 12 athletes were picked. The test subjects used a treadmill to run for 90 minutes before taking a four-hour break. Amid this recuperation 30 g/h of bee bread or a placebo were ingested by the subjects during the study. At 20-min intervals during this time, the tympanic temperature and heart rate were recorded. Plasma glucose, hemoglobin, and hematocrit levels in blood samples were measured. A treadmill experiment lasting 20 minutes was then completed by participants. 3.45 + 0.4 km vs. 3.24 + 0.4 km, respectively, was a significant increase in mileage from the bee bread study compared to the placebo trial. In comparison to the placebo experiment, the plasma glucose levels during recovery in the bee bread study were considerably higher. As a result of these findings, athletes' athletic performance appeared to be enhanced when bee bread was supplemented during the recuperation period. The use of bee bread supplementation was evaluated in a second research by Fadzel et al.

relating to athletes' running efficiency. Alternatively, the athletes received either 20 g of bee bread or a placebo. There was a 4-week washout period after the first trial run. The dosage was then continued for an additional 8 weeks prior to the second experimental trial. The individuals ran for 90 minutes at 60% of their maximum oxygen uptake during the experimental trials, then ran for 20 minutes. In addition to heart rate, the tests also measured oxygen consumption, ear temperature, subjective effort rate, ambient temperature, and relative humidity. Plasma glucose and free fatty acid concentrations were measured using blood testing. The study's findings revealed that there was no discernible distinction between the bee bread test and the placebo test.

Artificial Bee Bread

Because of their many biological activities and broad-based composition, hive products like honey and pollen have long been regarded as useful foods. Because of greater public knowledge of these products' nutritional and medicinal benefits, their consumption has recently expanded globally. This might result in significant commercial adulteration.

Bee bread is a product made from bees that contains a wide range of bioactive compounds, but it is still not widely known and is produced in limited quantities in apiaries due to difficult harvesting techniques and the beekeepers' conviction that bee bread reserves in the hives shouldn't be diminished to preserve the development of the colonies. Bee bread's demand has risen in the market relative to its production as a result of consumers' rising awareness of its health advantages. This has led to concerns among all bee product manufacturers about the possibility of adulteration. But the definition of the rules and standards for bee products is still in its early stages in the worldwide scientific community. Bee bread is currently difficult to prepare since there are no recognized standards to detect its falsification.

With reference to the composition previously covered in this work, the detection of fraudulent bee bread manipulations requires the combination of multiple techniques mainly based on the composition of pollen in bee bread, including the identification of the floral origin of the bee pollen (starter matrices to the bee bread production) by a palynological survey and the spectroscopic determination of the chemical composition of the bee bread, notably its vitamins (vitamin C, vitamin E, and β-carotene), amino acids, and fatty acids (taking into consideration the relationship between the botanical origin and chemical composition of bee pollen). Recent times have seen the application of sophisticated foodomics technology to define food products and have been applied to bee bread and other bee products to assess authenticity, safety, and quality issues and to determine the bioactive To identify the bioactive chemicals present and their biological functions, as well as to consider concerns of quality, safety, and presence. In their review article, Kafantaris et al. provided a concise overview of the various approaches used to study bee bread, including genomics as a substitute for palynologic/microscopic determination of the botanical origin using the metabarcoding of Bee pollen and bee bread samples were used to get the DNA.. Proteins, enzymes, fatty acids, phenolic profiles, and carotenoid composition may all be identified utilizing the proteomics and metabolomics technologies, which can be carried out using GC-MS, HPLC-DAD, SDS-PAGE, 2D-electrophoresis, and MALDI-MS techniques. Metagenomics may also be used to look at the bacterial community in bee bread, particularly lactobacillus bacteria.

On the basis of this, we may draw the conclusion that the identification of the microbiome and biological characteristics of bee pollen, as well as its chemical and enzymatic composition, are required for its validity and traceability.

Chapter 4

The disorder of colony collapse

There aren't enough healthy adult bees within the hive, which is a symptom of colony collapse disorder (CCD), a condition that affects honeybee colonies. Despite the fact that the reason is unknown, experts believe that a number of variables may be at play. It suggests that the condition impairs the adult bees' navigational skills. Foraging for pollen, they leave the hive and never come back. In the hive, honey, pollen, and frequently signs of recent brood raising can all be seen. The brood nest may occasionally contain the queen and a few remaining surviving bees. Other symptoms of CCD include the slow stealing of honey from the dead colonies by nearby, healthy bee colonies common pests like tiny hive beetles and wax moths are invading at a lesser rate than usual. It seems that only European honeybees are impacted by the condition.

Economic consequences of colony loss.

A commercial beekeeper from Pennsylvania, U.S., who was overwintering his honeybee colonies in Florida, initially reported the inexplicable loss of honeybee colonies that became known as CCD in the fall of 2006. (Following investigations, it was discovered that beekeepers had been reporting mysterious colony losses for at least the preceding three years; comparable losses had also been documented in the late 19th and in various decades of the 20th centuries.) By February 2007, many significant commercial migratory beekeeping operations in the United States have reported CCD incidences, with some operators losing 50–90% of their colonies. Numerous of these more substantial businesses were wintering their colonies in California, Florida, Oklahoma, and Texas. By the end of February 2007, a few nonmigratory enterprises in the mid-Atlantic and Pacific Northwest regions of the United States had also reported the loss of more than half of their colonies. Initial examinations were challenging and unreliable due to the lack of dead bees in the afflicted hives. In the same year, significant honeybee losses were also reported in Canada, Portugal, Italy, Spain, Greece, Germany, Poland, France, and Switzerland. Beekeepers blamed CCD for almost one-third of the nation's yearly colony losses between 2006 and 2011, which averaged out to about 33 percent overall. In contemporary agriculture, beekeeping is essential. In addition to posing a threat to beekeeping enterprises that produce honey and offer pollination services, CCD also poses a hazard to the numerous crops that depend on honeybees for pollination, which could seriously hamper agricultural output. More than 90 commercially cultivated crops, including numerous fruits and vegetables, depend on the pollination services of beekeepers in the United States. According to estimates, the $15 billion yearly economic worth of American crops that rely on honeybee pollination. There were more than one million bee colonies needed to pollinate the $1.9 billion worth of California almond exports in 2006. (out of a total of about 2.6

million colonies in the United States). The beekeeping business faced a huge issue in providing the demand for pollination services since the number of accessible colonies for agricultural pollination in the country was declining.

Probable Reasons
The U.S. Department of Agriculture's
Agricultural Research Service coordinated
efforts to address the CCD epidemic through
surveys and data collecting, sample analysis, and
mitigation and preventive measures There were
several different hypothesized causes of CCD.
They included chemical contamination of colony
food supplies or beeswax; poisoning from
pesticides, such as nicotine-based insecticides
known as neonicotinoids (whose use has been
prohibited in some countries); a potential lack of
genetic diversity in colonies; and infection of
colonies by pathogens or parasites, such as
known honeybee parasites like the single-celled
microsporidians (parasitic fungus) Nosema
ceranae and N. (Varroa destructor).

Impacts on the health of honeybees
By weakening bees' immune systems and
making colonies more vulnerable to illness,
colony stress may be a factor in CCD. The lack
of plants that produce nectar and pollen, the use
of honeybees to pollinate crops that provide little

nutritional value for bees, the overcrowding of honeybee colonies, the repetitive long-distance transportation of colonies for pollination or honey production, and the exposure of honeybees to pesticides and parasites are all potential sources of stress. So it stands to reason that efforts to enhance honeybee health may also help to lessen colony stress. During seasons of low nectar, low pollen, or bad weather, honeybee health may be enhanced by the development and use of better nutritional supplements. For potential early warning indicators of colony health problems that might cause or contribute to CCD, several significant migratory activities have undergone routine sampling. The use of genetic stocks that exhibit mite resistance, the application of fumigants such as formic-acid- or thymol-based products only when necessary, and feeding bees medications to prevent Nosema infections are some suggestions that have been offered to beekeepers to enhance honeybee health. The avoidance of reusing equipment that had come into contact with bee colonies that had perished from CCD was another suggestion.

Overview of the Bee Life Cycle

The egg, larva, pupal, and adult phases of the honey bee life cycle are separated into these four categories. Initial Stage: The Egg Stage The only bee capable of producing between 2,000 and 3,000 eggs in a single day is the queen bee. By the third day, the egg has shifted to an upright position before falling. In addition to fertilised eggs, the queen bee also lays unfertilized eggs. Queen bees or female bees develop from the fertilised egg. Male bees, sometimes known as drone bees, are created when the unfertilized egg hatches. Phase 2: The Larval Phase Three days after the egg turns into a larva and six days after the egg is deposited in the beehive, a worker bee may be distinguished from the queen bee. During their first three days as larvae, the "royal jelly" is provided to all the larvae, including the female bees, the workers, and the drone bees. During this phase, the larva sheds its skin several times. The female larvae, which develop into a queen bee, are the only ones afterwards given royal jelly. To protect and aid in the larvae's development into a pupa, the worker bees seal the top of the cell with beeswax. Phase 3, known as the pupal stage, is when the bee has acquired wings, eyes, legs, and little body hair, giving it a look that is very similar to that of an adult bee. The emerging adult bee chews its way out of the closed-cell after the pupa has reached adulthood in stage four. From the egg stage until adulthood, the queen bee takes 16 days. Drone bees grow into adult bees in 24 days, whereas worker bees need 18 to 22 days to reach full development.

Conclusion The pollination process is mostly made possible by honey bees. When pollinating, honey bees may fly at a speed of around 20 mph, while returning to the beehive with nectar they have collected at a speed of about 17 mph. The pollination process is more effective and

efficient as a whole because of this precise
reason. One of the tastiest dietary ingredients,
bee, wouldn't be available to us for a very long
time without honey bees sharing pollen.